I0831064

Around Venice

Text by Daniela Celli

Illustrations by Laura Re

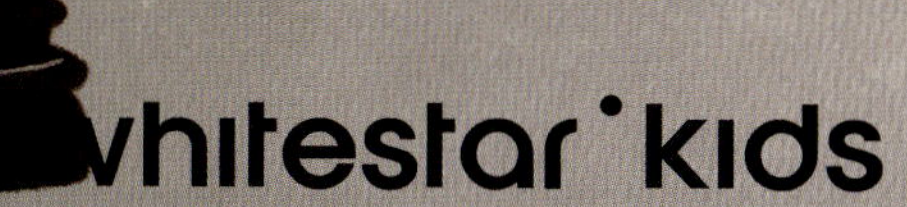

FOR PARENTS

I could give you innumerable reasons why you should visit Venice with your children: To begin with, there are no cars, and moving by gondolas and *vaporetti* already feels like an adventure, plus many museums offer guided tours designed for families, the islands of the lagoon are a galaxy of colors, and among the small piazzas, *calli*, and *campielli*, there is always a cat to pet. But there is another reason, shown by reversing the title of a marvelous book by Štěpán Zavřel, *A Dream in Venice*:

VENICE IS A DREAM: A CITY MADE OF WATER THAT DOES NOT FOLLOW COMMON RULES: IT RIPPLES, REFLECTS, IMAGINES.
IT IS SUCH A DIFFERENT WORLD THAT EVERYTHING SEEMS POSSIBLE.

What better place therefore to imagine being pirates, adventurers, or explorers? The four itineraries included in this guide will aid in sparking your imagination and transforming your trip into an extraordinary adventure.
Hand it to your young explorers and let them guide you along the foundations and bridges of the lagoon, discovering stories, legends, interesting facts, and the magic that surprisingly floods every *sestiere*.

To the Monster of my heart that like me believes in the magic of dreams.
With all the love of the world,

Daniela Celli

"BON ZORNO", GOOD MORNING, CHILDREN: LET ME INTRODUCE MYSELF!

My name is Sior Leo, and I am happy to take you along to discover my beautiful city! We will explore Venice's *sestieri*, or districts, on the hunt for interesting stories and facts, and will set sail for brightly colored islands and taste delicious delicacies because, I confess, I am a rather hungry lion. We will have lots of fun together! Venice is certainly not just any city! Think about the fact that it is on water, and instead of cars, gondolas and *vaporetti* dart "on her roads." And did you know that there are more bridges here than black rhinoceroses in the savanna, each with a name, often a bizarre one, that hides legends and features?

I have prepared FOUR DIFFERENT ITINERARIES for you that will lead us along *calli* and *campielli*, buildings that look like castles, squares, and secret gardens. Each itinerary starts with A MAP, where you will find the planned stops depicted next to some interesting facts. In addition, between one adventure and the next, I have organized some SMALL GAMES so ... sharpen your eyes!

NOW, WHAT DO YOU THINK? SHALL WE START?

CONTENTS

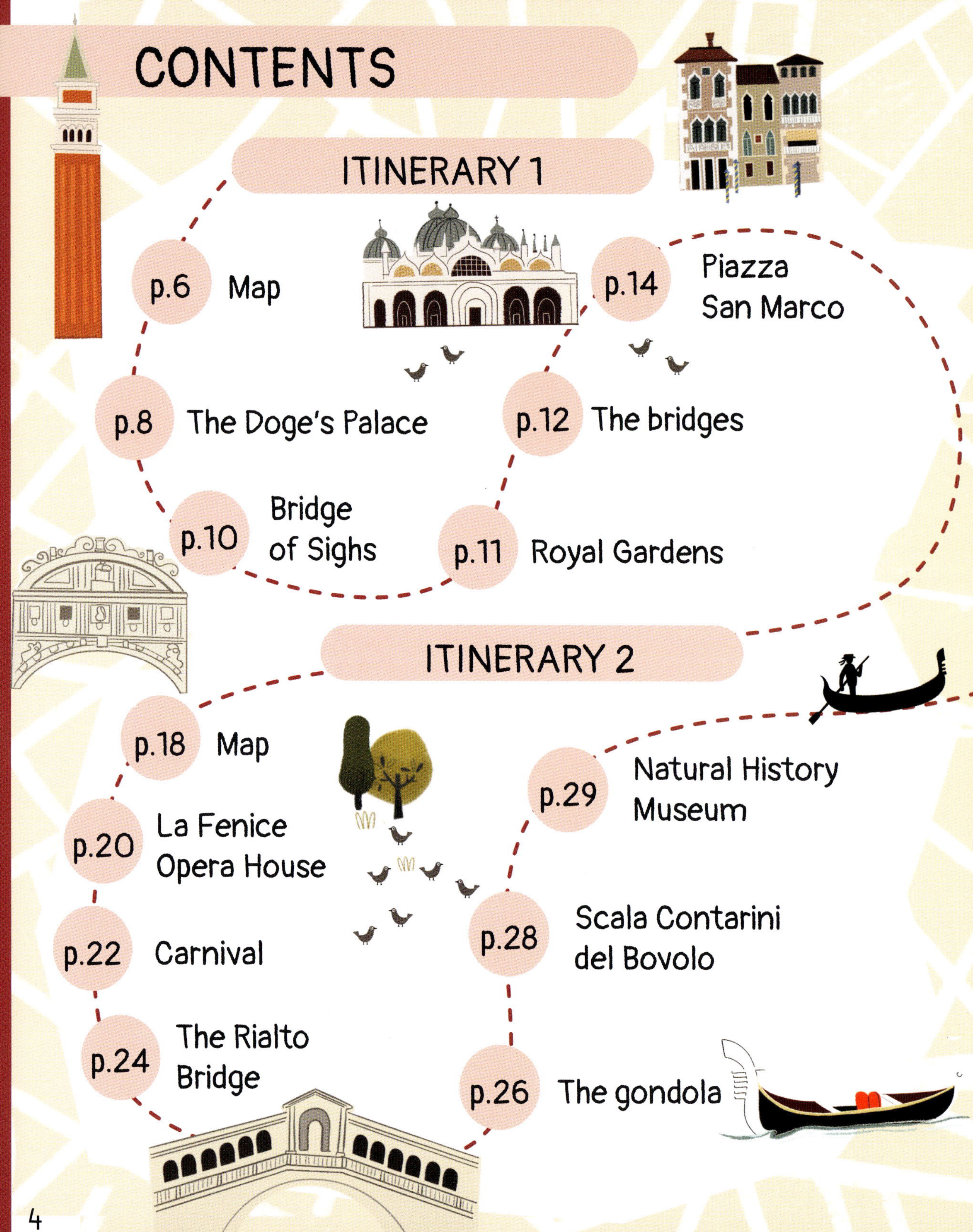

ITINERARY 3
p.30 Map
p.32 Venice Biennale
p.34 Arsenal
p.35 The Naval Museum
p.36 The Lido of Venice
p.38 Legends
ITINERARY 4
p.40 Map
p.42 Giudecca
p.43 San Giorgio Maggiore
p.44 Burano
Murano p.46
Goodbye!
p.47

VENICE

Bondì, good morning boys and girls, and welcome to Venice!

ITINERARY 1

Today we will spend the day exploring the SAN MARCO *sestiere*. What are the *SESTIERI*? They are the six neighborhoods into which the city is divided. We will start from a PALACE that looks like a castle but hides secret prisons and bridges, we will look out of the little windows of a BRIDGE, sighing like the prisoners who walked it, and we will relax in a wonderful GREEN OASIS. And finally we will discover all the secrets of one of the most beautiful squares in the WORLD.

ARE YOU READY TO GO?

- **How to find your way?**

In Venice there are no "roads," "streets," or "squares" (except one!) because many things are named differently. Here is a little help to navigate better!

- *Calle*: street
- *Calletta*: very narrow street
- *Ruga*: long and important *calle*
- *Campo*: square
- *Campiello*: small square
- *Fondamenta*: road that skirts the canal
- *Sottoportego*: road that passes under a building

- **Venetian toponymy (street names)**

Within every *sestiere* the house numbers start with number one and continue to the last one. You may find houses with the number 6423 or 5558.

POOR LETTER CARRIERS!

VENICE LAGOON

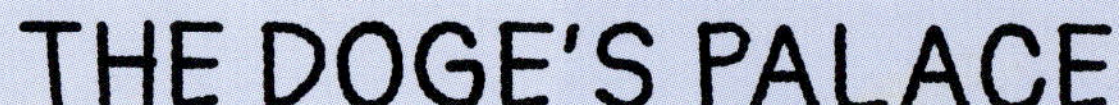

THE DOGE'S PALACE

The first stop of our trip truly seems to have come out of a fairy tale.

The Doge's Palace, with its splendid porticoes of arches and columns, resembles a majestic CASTLE SUSPENDED ON THE WATER. It was here that a few centuries ago the *doges* lived; they were very important people who governed the Republic of Venice. In addition to the doge's apartment, the building also housed the law courts and prisons, where those sentenced for the most serious crimes were locked up.

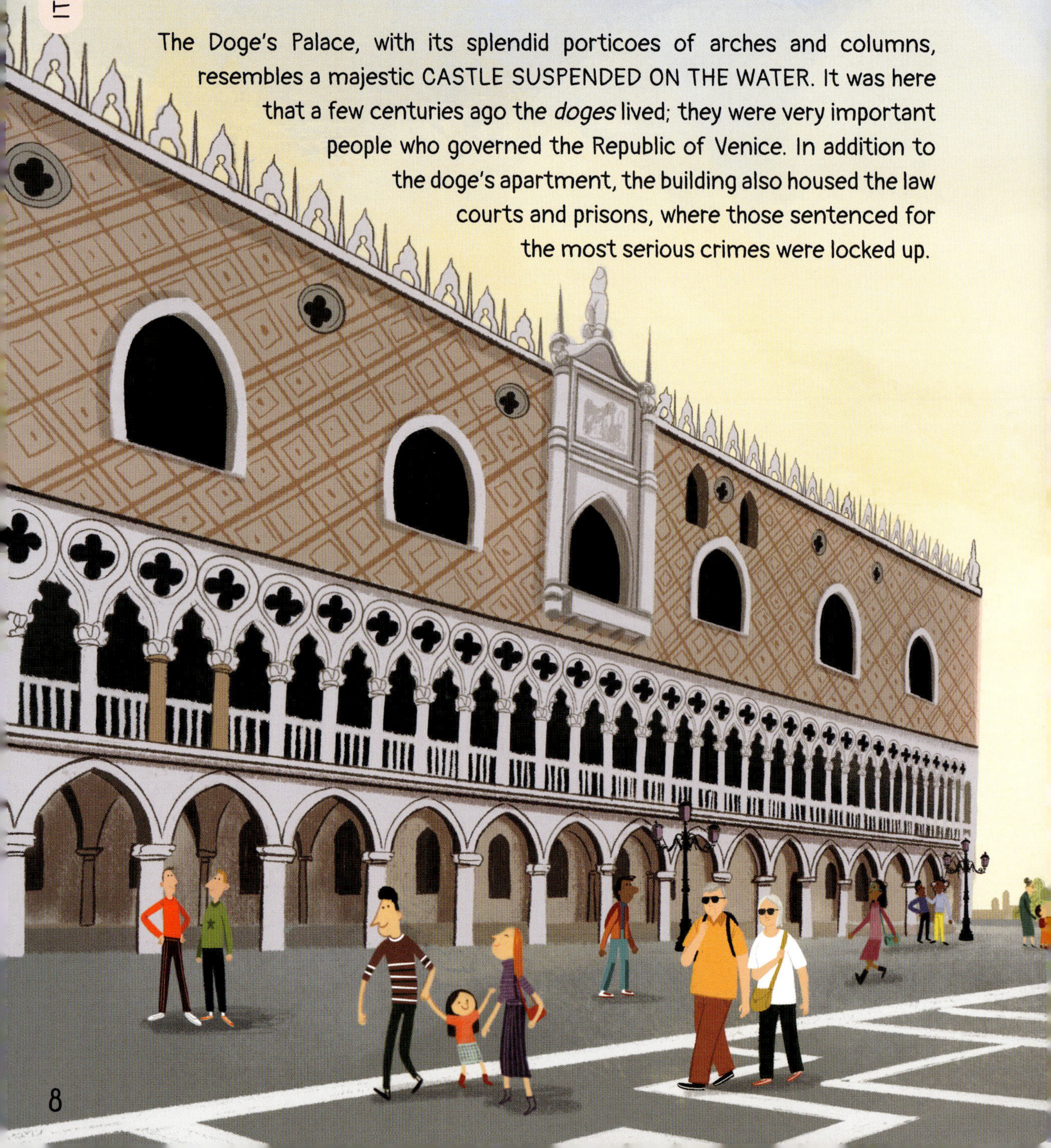

• Find the intruders
By carefully observing the beautiful white columns that look out on the square, you will see that two of them stand out because of their REDDISH COLOR.

IT'S SAID THAT FROM HERE THE DOGE ISSUED DEATH SENTENCES AMONG THE RED MARBLE OF VERONA, WHICH RECALLED THE BLOOD OF THE CONDEMNED.

• The *Bocche de Leon*
What are those strange lion faces scattered about, with an opening for the mouth?

THEY ARE BIZARRE MAILBOXES THAT WERE USED TO SECRETLY REPORT THOSE WHO HAD COMMITTED A CRIME!

THE BRIDGE OF SIGHS

Follow me, children. We are about to enter a place that is a little sinister and a little mysterious...

Built over 400 years ago, the Bridge of Sighs connects the Doge's Palace to the prisons through two narrow corridors that straddle the canal. It was through here that the condemned passed once they were judged guilty, and when looking through the little windows they sighed for the freedom they lost, so you can fully understand how it got its name.

• **The Lovers' Bridge**
Despite its sad purpose, an old legend says that if two sweethearts passing in a gondola under the bridge kiss, they will stay together forever. ISN'T IT ROMANTIC?

IF YOU WANT TO KNOW OTHER INTERESTING FACTS ABOUT THE VENETIAN BRIDGES TURN THE PAGE.

THE ROYAL GARDENS

A little relaxation in the botanical oasis of Venice.

Commissioned by NAPOLEON and much loved by EMPRESS SISI, the Royal Gardens are a marvelous green corner hidden between the Grand Canal and Piazza San Marco.

THE MOST MAGICAL TIME TO VISIT THEM IS SPRING, WHEN THE WISTERIA THAT WRAPS THE PERGOLAS TRANSFORMS THEM INTO A FABULOUS FLOWERED, PERFUMED CORRIDOR.

- **Botanical photographic hunt**

The gardens are spread over 1.23 acres (5,000 square meters) and include numerous species of PLANTS and TREES. Look for the large vases with bitter oranges, figs, loquats, and pomegranates. Photograph the most beautiful flowers that you find depending on the season. I adore roses, tulips, daffodils, and the wonderful *Agapanthus*!

THE BRIDGES OF VENICE

A city that floats on water has to have hundreds of bridges!
The center of Venice includes a total of 121 islands, connected by 435 bridges! Some are very small, like the Ponte de la Toleta, or very large, like the Ponte dell'Accademia.
There are very ancient bridges, like the Rialto Bridge built long ago in 1265, and new bridges like the Solesin. There are wooden and iron bridges, public and private bridges, used by citizens to get to their homes.
And they all have a story to tell.

LET'S SEE THE STRANGEST!

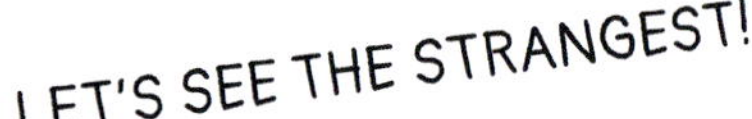

• Ponte di Paglia

Always very crowded because of the beautiful view of the Bridge of Sighs, it owes its name, the Straw Bridge, to the boats moored here to unload and load straw.
In the past this material was widely used to insulate roofs and to feed donkeys and horses.

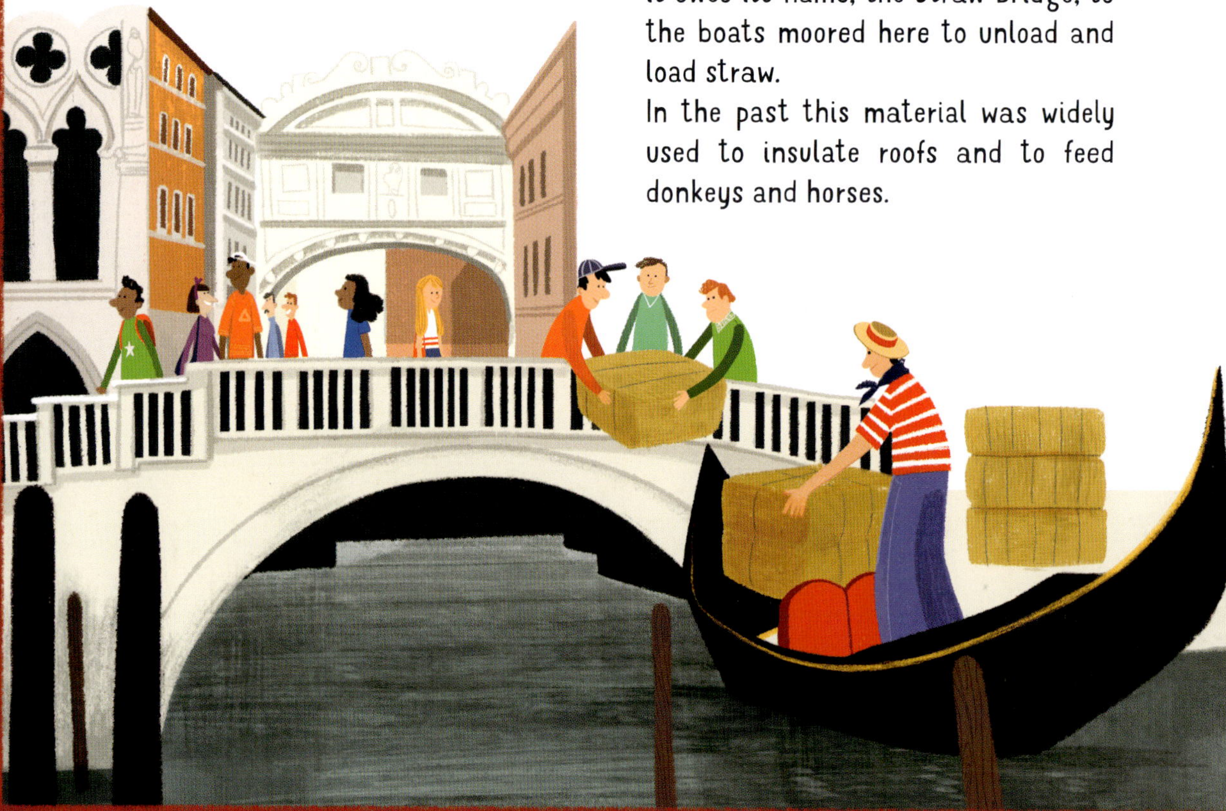

• Ponte degli Scalzi

Located near the station, it is one of the four bridges that cross the Grand Canal. Its funny name does not mean that you have to cross it with bare feet (this is what *scạlzi* means) but comes from the nearby Santa Maria di Nazareth Church belonging to the religious order of the BAREFOOT Carmelites.

• Ponte dei Pugni

This small stone bridge is located in the *sestiere* of Dorsoduro, and it inherited its name from an ancient Venetian tradition: the war of fists.

At one time the bridge did not have railings, and members of two different factions challenged each other, trying to toss their rivals into the canal!

PIAZZA SAN MARCO

Welcome to one of the most beautiful squares in the world!

Considered the symbol of Venice, Piazza San Marco is the heart of the city. It is almost two soccer fields long and has the elegant shape of a trapezoid surrounded by splendid MONUMENTS. In addition to the large area enclosed between the Procuratie, the Basilica, the Clock Tower, and the Campanile, it includes the Piazzetta di San Marco on which the Doge's Palace looks out and the Piazzetta dei Leoncini.

- **La Piazzetta dei Leoncini**

But why are there three steps up? As the centuries passed, many areas were raised to prevent them from being flooded by high water. Safe in the center, there is the well that provided drinking water to inhabitants.

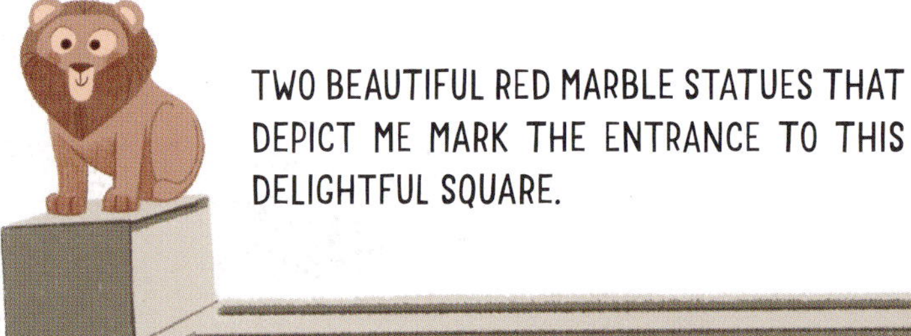

TWO BEAUTIFUL RED MARBLE STATUES THAT DEPICT ME MARK THE ENTRANCE TO THIS DELIGHTFUL SQUARE.

• The only square of the city

Piazza San Marco is the only real square of the city. The others, depending on the size are called *campi*, *campielli* or *corti* (courtyards).

OTHER INTERESTING FACTS ABOUT PIAZZA SAN MARCO!

• ***La Fiera della Sensa* (Feast of the Ascension)**

By looking at the paving in Piazza San Marco, you'll immediately notice that it is covered by many white outlines. WHAT ARE THEY? Well, in the past, during the month of May, the *Fiera della Sensa* was held—a fair that lasted two weeks during which lots of goods were sold, from perfumes and velvet to ceramics, spices, and even animals.

THE OUTLINES SERVED TO DEMARCATE THE SPACES RESERVED FOR VENDORS.

• **A lucky misunderstanding**

Inside the Basilica there is the extraordinary *Pala d'oro* (Golden Altarpiece), a very ancient Byzantine work that decorates the altar and is studded with precious stones.

BUT HOW DID THE VENETIANS GUARD SUCH A VALUABLE TREASURE? According to legend, it involves a lucky misunderstanding. When Napoleon tried to take it away he was told that it was *ex vero* (real), but he thought that it was made of glass and left it there!

• A valuable treasure

The majestic Saint Mark's Basilica is more than a thousand years old and is also known by the name "Church of Gold." In fact, inside, in addition to the legendary Pala, there is a fabulous TREASURE made up of almost 300 objects, many of which were made with valuable materials and set with precious stones.

• The master of the house

Called by the Venetians *El parón di casa*, the St. Mark's Campanile, 323.5 feet (98.6 meters) high, is one of the tallest bell towers in Italy.

TODAY YOU CAN REACH THE BELFRY BY ELEVATOR. THE VIEW IS MAGNIFICENT FROM UP THERE!

Friends, follow me. A new itinerary awaits us!

ITINERARY 2

Today we will begin by visiting a theater with a legendary name. We will discover the scariest masks of CARNIVAL, we will take a ride on the most famous boat of Venice, and we will climb up a long spiral staircase to admire the city from above.

Finally, we will walk under gigantic whales and around a dinosaur skeleton over 23 feet (7 meters) long!

BUT WHAT DO YOU THINK ABOUT FIRST STOPPING FOR *CICCHETTI*?

CARNIVAL

• Visit the *bacari*

Cicchetti are small snacks (*ciccum* in Latin means "small quantity") that are eaten in the *bacari*, typical Venetian taverns. Usually these SNACKS are perfect as appetizers, but it is fun to dine *cicchettando* (by snacking), going from *bacaro* to *bacaro*!

• Spoiled for choice

There are lots of types of *cicchetti*: meat, fish, with cheese, salami, or vegetables, hot or cold. HERE ARE A FEW:

- *Baccalà mantecato*: creamed cod and oil served on bread or polenta.
- *Trippa rissa*: strips of fried tripe.
- *Schie e Polenta*: shrimp from the lagoon fried or boiled and served with a creamy polenta.
- *Zeólete in agro e dólze*: spring onions in sweet and sour sauce.

LA FENICE OPERA HOUSE

"La laaaaa, la la la la la la la la laaaaa..."
Umm, sorry children, but I love to sing!

Inaugurated in 1792 during the *Fiera della Sensa*, La Fenice Theater is the principal opera house of Venice and one of the most prestigious in the world. On its splendid stage, famous lyric operas such as *La Traviata* by Giuseppe Verdi were produced for the first time.

WHAT DO YOU THINK? SHOULD WE VISIT IT?

• An apt name

The theater bears the name of the phoenix, a legendary bird capable of rising from its own ashes. In 1836 the theater was devastated by flames caused by a defective stove, and just slightly more than a hundred years later, another fire destroyed it completely.

LIKE THE PHOENIX, THE OPERA HOUSE "RETURNED TO LIFE" AND WAS FAITHFULLY REBUILT, RECAPTURING ALL ITS SPLENDOR.

• Entry by water

Today, the main entrance of the theater is the one on Campo San Fantin, but at one time it was usual to go to the Fenice by boat! In fact, the rear entrance, like many Venetian palaces, faces the water.

During Carnival, the Fenice stage turns into a ballroom, and some spectators arrive by gondola wearing masks.

ON THE SUBJECT OF MASKS, TURN THE PAGE IF YOU WANT TO LEARN MORE ABOUT THE FAMOUS VENETIAN CARNIVAL!

LET'S DISCOVER INTERESTING FACTS ABOUT CARNIVAL!

• Good morning, *Siora* mask!

The Venetian Carnival has very ancient origins. In the past it lasted a full SIX WEEKS, and it was a way to grant the inhabitants a period of great entertainment. In addition to the celebrations and the BALLS in the palaces, all the citizens wore MASKS to conceal their identity, men and women, rich and poor, without any distinction.

• The flight of the angel

This ancient tradition involves a person dressed as an angel launching from the St. Mark's Campanile and sliding down a hanging cable.

MY, I COULD NEVER DO THAT. I AM AFRAID OF HEIGHTS!

ARE YOU CURIOUS TO FIND OUT ABOUT SOME TRADITIONAL MASKS?

• The plague doctor

Maybe it is the pointed beak or the completely black costume, but this mask frightens me a little. In reality, in the past the BEAK did not have any monstrous purpose but served as container for MEDICINAL HERBS.

In this way, the doctors that wore it hoped not to get infected by the terrible disease that affected Venice twice: the PLAGUE.

• The *Bauta*

It is one of the most ancient costumes and includes a white mask, wider in the lower section so as to be able to eat and drink freely.

IT WAS ALSO USED AT TIMES OTHER THAN CARNIVAL, TO BE ABLE TO GET AROUND THE CITY INCOGNITO, AND IT WAS MANDATORY FOR MARRIED WOMEN WHO WERE GOING TO THE THEATER!

WHAT WOULD YOU LIKE TO DRESS UP AS?

THE RIALTO BRIDGE

Siore e Siori, Ladies and Gentlemen,
here is one of the most famous bridges of Venice!

The Rialto Bridge is the oldest of the four bridges that cross the Grand Canal, the main canal that divides the historic center into two parts.
Coincidentally, it was designed by a sculptor named ANTONIO... DA PONTE ("Bridge")!
Almost 500 years ago, he managed the difficult task of creating a stone structure that was high enough to allow large boats that were carrying merchandise to the nearby market to pass beneath it. To support it, as many as 12,000 wooden stakes were stuck in the soil underwater.

- **Not just a passage**

The Rialto Bridge is an "inhabited bridge." In addition to allowing people to pass over, it houses structures where various activities are carried out.

"HIDDEN" WITHIN IT ARE TWO ROWS OF SHOPS, WITH A TOTAL OF 24 STORES!

Discovery quest

1 Bauta
5 seagulls
1 little dog
1 female gondolier

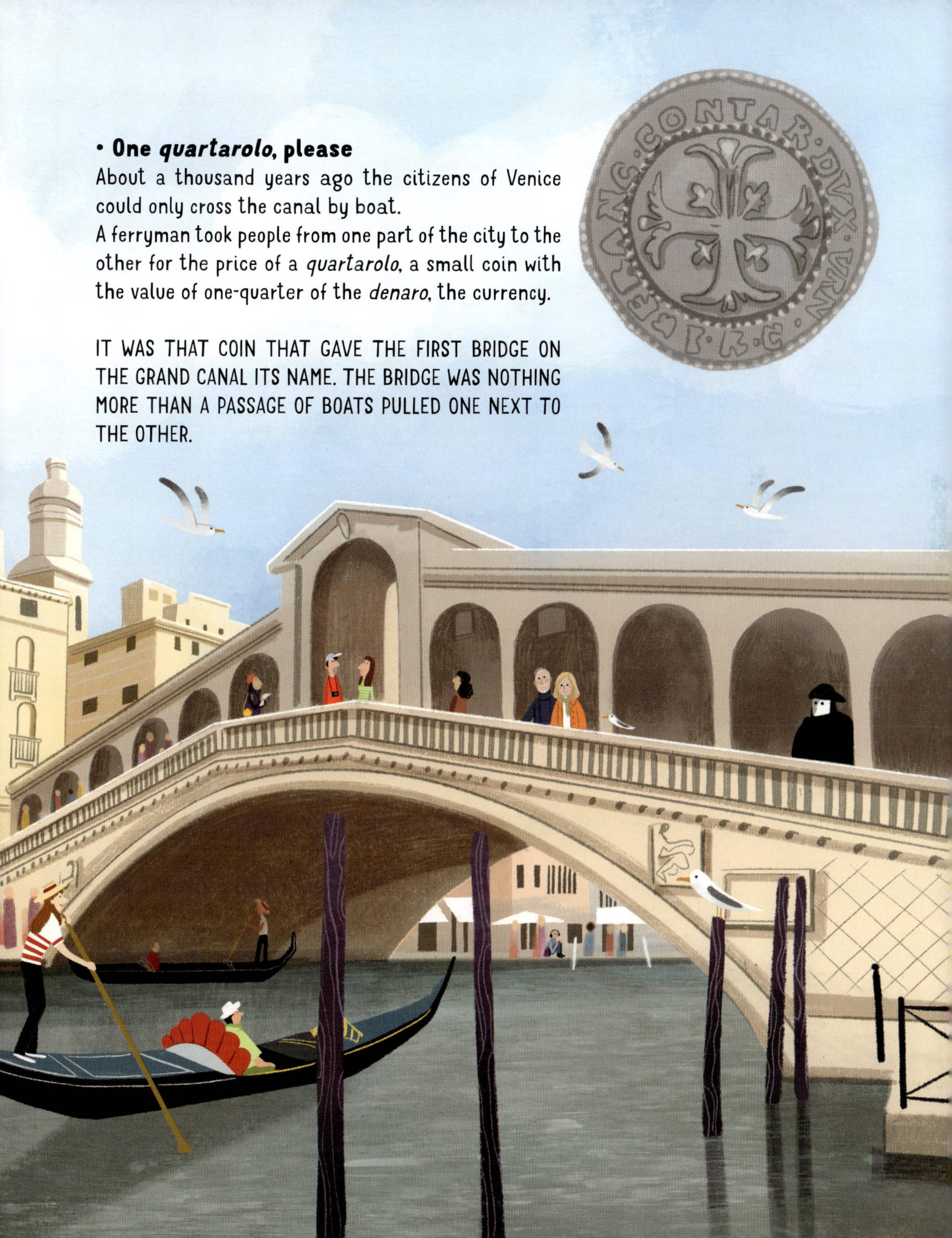

• One *quartarolo*, please

About a thousand years ago the citizens of Venice could only cross the canal by boat.
A ferryman took people from one part of the city to the other for the price of a *quartarolo*, a small coin with the value of one-quarter of the *denaro*, the currency.

IT WAS THAT COIN THAT GAVE THE FIRST BRIDGE ON THE GRAND CANAL ITS NAME. THE BRIDGE WAS NOTHING MORE THAN A PASSAGE OF BOATS PULLED ONE NEXT TO THE OTHER.

Let's discover some interesting facts about the legendary Venetian gondola.

• A boat that is unique in the world

The gondola is a boat that has been used to navigate VENICE'S CANALS for almost a thousand years.

In the past it was the main means of transportation, and every well-to-do family owned at least one.

Today it is used mostly to take tourists around. It is 36 feet (11 meters) long, weighs as much as a large horse, and is composed of 280 pieces made with 8 types of wood.

THANKS TO ITS ELONGATED SHAPE, IT MOVES EASILY THROUGH THE WATERWAYS AND MANAGES TO PASS UNDER SMALL BRIDGES, BUT THE GONDOLIER'S EXPERIENCE AND ABILITY IS NECESSARY.

• The secret significance of the *fero da prora*

On the front of every gondola is the so-called *fero da prora*, or *FERRO DI PRUA*, a metal blade that serves to balance the weight of the gondolier.
Its particular shape has a hidden meaning: The six "teeth" facing forward represent the six Venetian *sestieri*; the tooth facing backward is the *Giudecca*; the top is the *Doge's Hat*; the small arch is the Rialto Bridge; three embroideries are the islands of Murano, Burano, and Torcello; and the large "S" is the fabulous Grand Canal!

Giudecca
Doge's Hat
Rialto Bridge
San Marco
San Paolo
Santa Croce
Castello
Dorsoduro
Cannaregio
Grand Canal

• Strategic asymmetry

HAVE YOU NOTICED THAT THE LEFT SIDE OF THE GONDOLA IS WIDER THAN THE RIGHT SIDE?

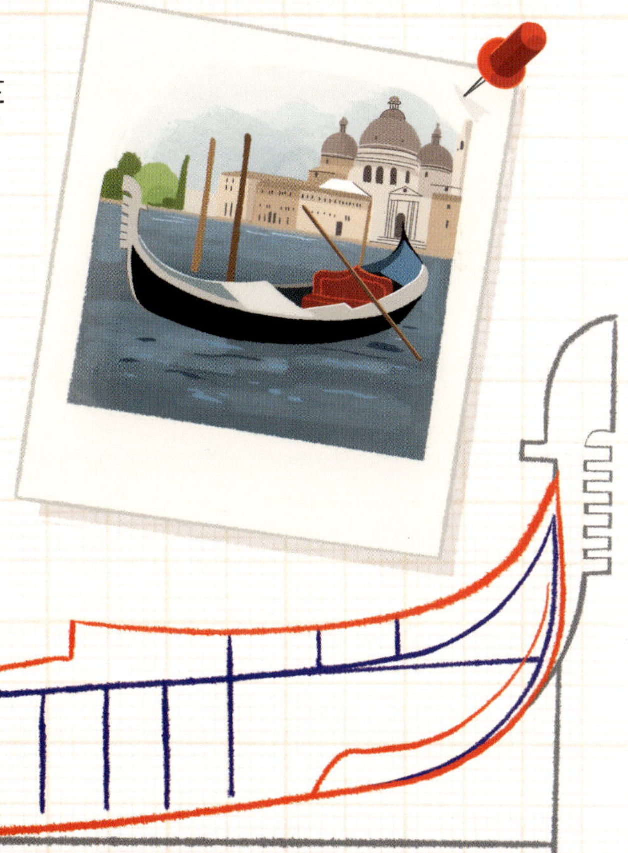

No, my friends, it is not a mistake of the *squeraiol* (the manufacturer), but a characteristic that keeps them tilted and allows the gondoliers to row more easily Venetian-style—in other words standing upright in the stern (the rear part) and using a single oar!

SCALA CONTARINI DEL BOVOLO

Let's go up one of the hidden jewels of Venice

In 1499 an ancient and noble Venetian family called CONTARINI had a lavish staircase built to further embellish their palace, which was already covered with frescoes and decorations. Just under 85.3 feet (26 meters) high, it is a spiral of 80 steps that wind up the inside of a tower punctuated by arches. *Bovolo* in Venetian means SLOWPOKE, or better, SNAIL!

NOW FOLLOW ME! FROM THE TOP YOU GET A MARVELOUS VIEW OVER VENICE!

- **A nighttime ride**

An old legend says that PIETRO CONTARINI had the external staircase built so he could reach his bedroom on horseback.

NATURAL HISTORY MUSEUM

From palace of merchants to museum

After having been the residence of Ottoman merchants for centuries, the *Fontego dei turchi*, a splendid palace decorated with battlements and arches that faces the Grand Canal, today houses the Natural History Museum of Venice. Its symbol, depicted in one of the many tiles on the facade, is a bird catching a fish.

• Whales, fossils, and the mysteries of the lagoon

The museum is a magical kingdom in which we can walk among the giants of the sea in the gallery of whales, take a trip back in time by turning into paleontologists on the hunt for dinosaurs, admire the collections of the great Venetian explorers, and discover all the secrets of the lagoon.

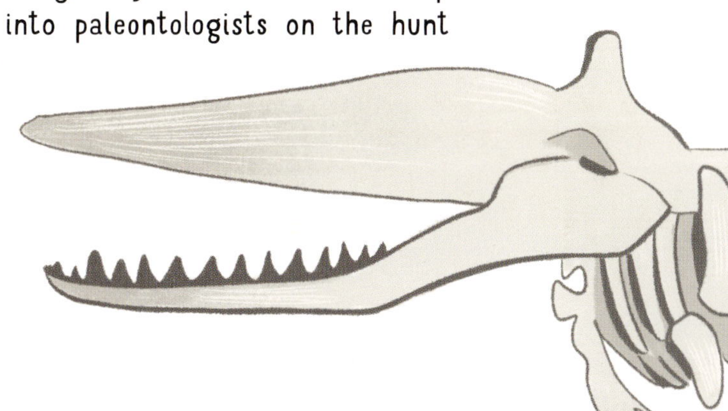

Are you ready for a new adventure?

ITINERARY 3

Today we will start the day by taking a small TOUR OF THE WORLD! Then we will go on a discovery of the secrets of ships and galleys and, after getting on a *vaporetto*, we will disembark on a very narrow island. Here will get on a bike and, pushed by the wind, we will pedal to the lighthouse. Finally, while we are doing some birdwatching I will tell you some lovely legends about witches, sorcerers, and monsters of the lagoon.

BUT BEFORE GETTING BACK ONBOARD, WHAT WOULD YOU THINK ABOUT STOPPING IN TWO EXTRAORDINARY LIBRARIES?

- ***Sullaluna* (On the Moon)**
Spread along a canal of Cannaregio there is a magical place—a library overflowing with magnificent illustrated books where we can sit at little tables that almost brush the water to taste delicious snacks, cakes, and canapés, and fabulous hot chocolates!

- **High Water**
In this library located in the heart of the Castello *sestiere* you will find cats that sleep in the most unusual places, like barrels, benches, and even a gondola brimming with volumes, and *dulcis in fundo*, a real staircase made of books on which you can climb to look at the canal.

ISN'T IT INCREDIBLE?

VENICE BIENNALE

Let's go around the world through art!

The Venice Biennale of Art is one of the most important international events of contemporary art.
Since its first event in 1895, the traditional site of the exhibition is the Napoleonic gardens, a splendid park that houses theme-based pavilions where the artists exhibit their works.

YOU WILL FIND ENORMOUS PAINTINGS AND STRANGE STATUES, GIGANTIC HEADS OF DRAGONS, AND EVEN INSTALLATIONS THAT MOVE ON THEIR OWN!

• **An open-air museum**
Created by Napoleon in 1807, the gardens are the largest green area of the historic center. There are 29 pavilions here that can be visited when the exhibitions are open.

SOME ARE VERITABLE WORKS OF ART THAT TRANSFORM THE GARDENS INTO AN EXTRAORDINARY MUSEUM "EN PLEIN AIR."

• Around the world in 29 pavilions

The pavilions are exhibit spaces that are assigned to ALL THE COUNTRIES that participate in the BIENNALE; visiting them is a little like taking a trip around the world!

IN ADDITION, EVERY NEW EDITION OF THE BIENNALE HAS A SPECIFIC THEME THAT THE ARTISTS MUST REFER TO—FROM FANTASTIC ANIMALS TO ARTIFICIAL INTELLIGENCE.

WHAT THEME WOULD YOU SUGGEST?

ARSENAL

Have you ever visited a shipyard?

The ARSENAL is the place where all the ships of the military and merchant fleet of the Republic of Venice were built. At one time, 16,000 specialized workers, called *arsenalotti*, worked there, masters who with great ability built galleys, merchant ships, and other ships for warfare. Since the activity at the shipyard had to remain SECRET, the arsenal was surrounded by 1.8 miles (3 kilometers) of high red brick walls on which a land door and a water door opened.

• **The Dry Docks**

In the *Darsena* it is possible to see up close the fascinating *dry docks*, which are like ARTIFICIAL SWIMMING POOLS that, when emptied of water, allowed the hulls of the large iron ships to be "dry" for necessary maintenance.

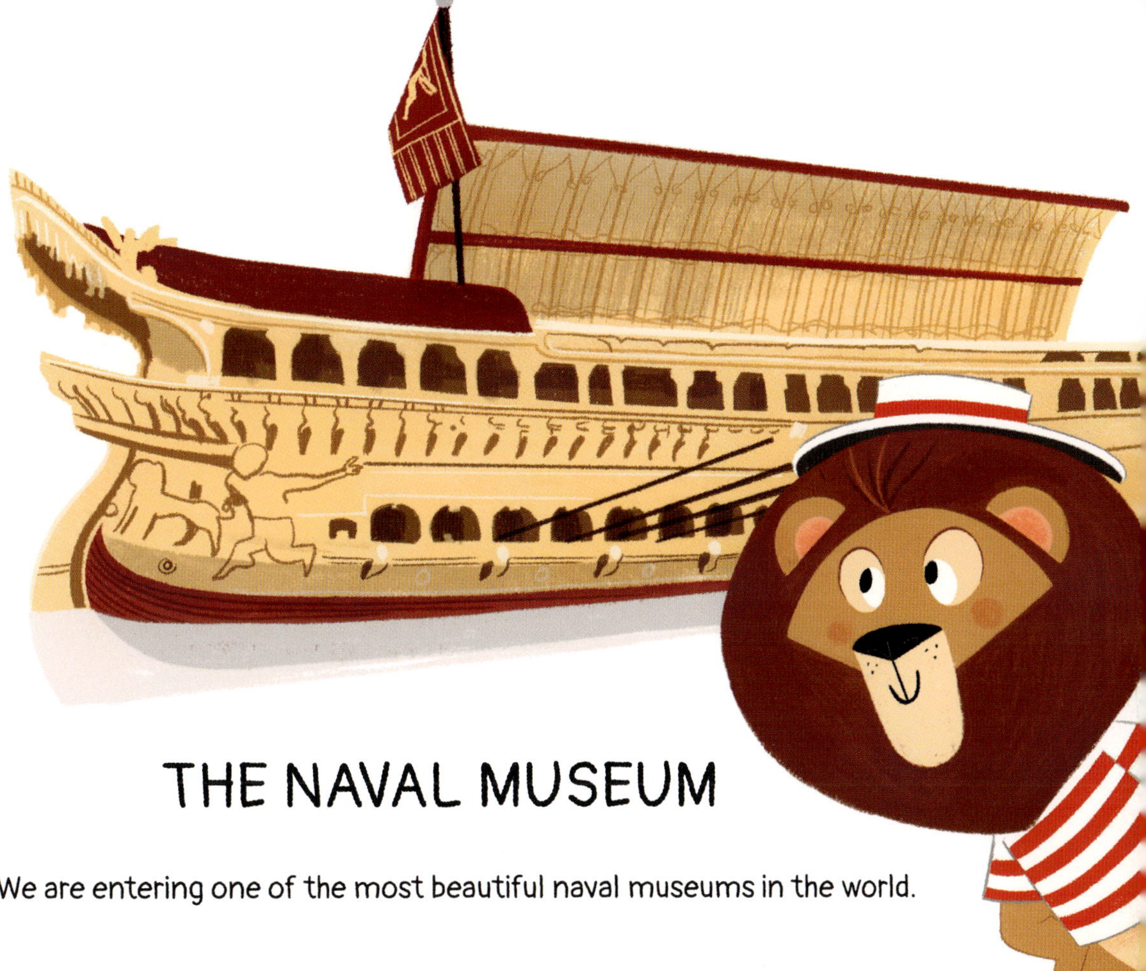

THE NAVAL MUSEUM

We are entering one of the most beautiful naval museums in the world.

Visiting the MUNAV is like taking a magnificent trip through the glorious maritime history of Venice. At one time the building that houses it was a CITY GRANARY where GRAINS were stored for the production of biscuits, which were a type of cracker that was the main food of sailors.

• The treasure of Venice

The museum is organized on three levels and includes 40 rooms with ships, weapons, nautical instruments, historic memorabilia of the maritime world, and one of the treasures of Venice: the Bucentaur!

The Bucentaur is a large galley decorated with inlays and gilding, which the *doge* sailed during the ceremony of the *Festa della Sensa*. It owes its name to the *bucinatores*, the musicians that played the *buccina* (an instrument similar to the trumpet) announcing its arrival to the citizens.

THE LIDO OF VENICE

Let's get onboard, my brave ones, the island is waiting for us!

The Lido is a thin strip of land between the lagoon and the sea.
It is a real island, and to get there we must take one of the *vaporetti*, the boats that are used in Venice as public transportation.
THE ISLAND IS 7.45 MILES (12 KILOMETERS) LONG AND DOTTED WITH BEACHES.
There are three beautiful nature oases where various kinds of birds nest, a pine forest, an old airport, and a lighthouse.

SHALL WE TAKE BIKES TO GET THERE?

LITTLE RINGED
PLOVER

LITTLE TERN

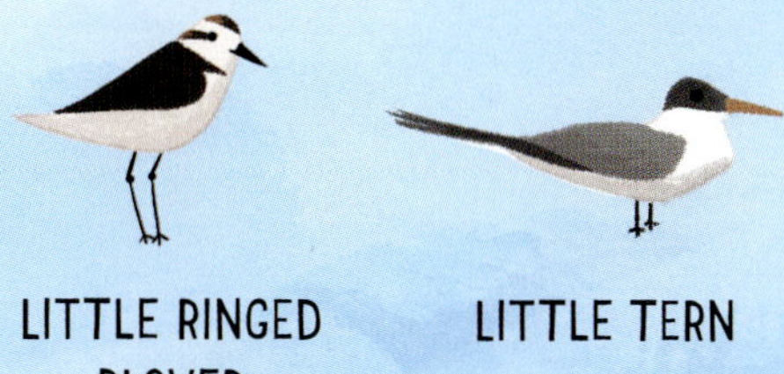

• Birdwatching

On nice days, when the sea is calm, it is easy to see little ringed plovers and little terns.

DON'T FORGET TO BRING BINOCULARS WITH YOU!

• The San Nicolò Lighthouse

In the northernmost part of the Lido, at the end of a breakwater that is about 1.8 miles (3 kilometers) long, there is a lovely red lighthouse. It is an enchanting place where you can breathe in the scent of the sea and enjoy a magnificent view.

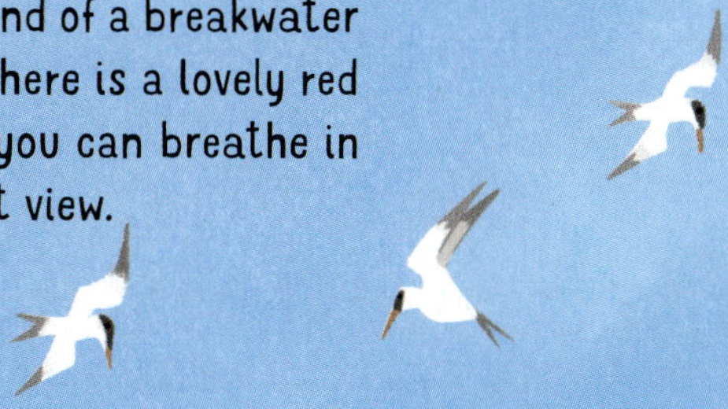

YOU SHOULD SEE HOW
BEAUTIFUL THE SUNSET IS!

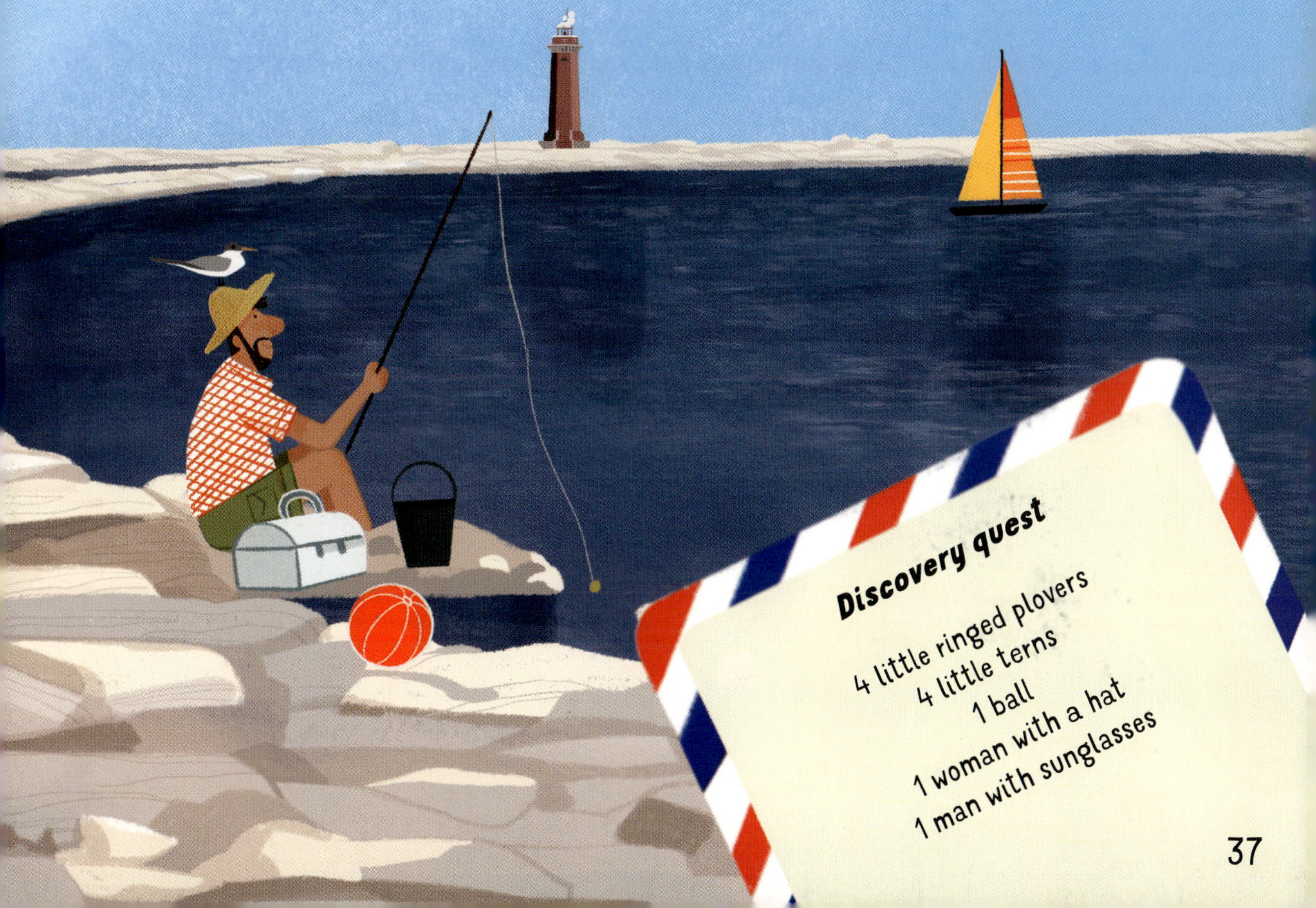
Discovery quest
4 little ringed plovers
4 little terns
1 ball
1 woman with a hat
1 man with sunglasses

LET'S DISCOVER SOME INTERESTING FACTS ABOUT VENETIAN LEGENDS

• The stone merchants of Palazzo Mastelli

In Campo dei Mori there is a strange palace that once belonged to three brothers.
You can easily find it because of the CAMEL that decorates the facade. The three merchants had gotten rich by selling SPICES and FABRICS, but they did not always act honestly.

One day, while they were trying to cheat one of their client they exclaimed, "May God turn us into stone if this is not the best fabric in Venice!"
And so it was...

LOOK AROUND THE *CAMPO* FOR THE BROTHERS AND THEIR SERVANT, AND DO NOT FORGET TO TOUCH THE IRON NOSE OF SIOR RIOBA—THEY SAY IT BRINGS GOOD LUCK!

• The Time of the Witch

If passing along Dorsoduro, I suggest you enter the *Calle* della Toletta and look up, where you will see an old ALARM CLOCK hanging on the wall. It is said that this alarm clock served to mark the best hours to cast spells to a terrible witch.

EVERY TIME IT BREAKS IT MUST BE REPLACED, OTHERWISE SINISTER AND MYSTERIOUS EVENTS WILL OCCUR.

- **The lions of the Arsenal**

Along the walls that surround the arsenal, there are FOUR LIONS of white marble. The story goes that in the past, by brushing the writing etched on the stone, a SORCERER was able to bring them to life and unleash them on his enemies. But one day a man interrupted the evil spell by decapitating a beast before it turned back into stone.

GULP! IF YOU LOOK CLOSELY AT THE STATUES, YOU WILL NOTICE THAT ONE HEAD HAS BEEN REPLACED...

- **The monster of the black water**

They say that in a large hollow located under *Punta della Dogana*, a BIZARRE CREATURE with the body of a serpent and the head of a horse lives. By day, it stays hidden because it fears the gondoliers, but when it emerges on moonless nights, it blows so hard that it wraps the city in fog.

IF YOU WANT TO SEE IT EMERGE FROM THE WATER WITHOUT RUNNING INTO ANY RISK...

...YOU CAN FIND A LOVELY ANIMATED STATUE OF THE MONSTER IN THE MURANO GLASS MUSEUM!

ROAR!

Is it possible that we have already arrived at the last itinerary?

ITINERARY 4

Today a great adventure awaits us among the islands of the lagoon. We will land on GIUDECCA, which looks like a fish bone (but also a sleeping serpent), for a delicious mission; we will dock at SAN GIORGIO for a hunt for objects hidden in a labyrinth; we will slip into a box of colors in BURANO; and finally, after having tasted sweets and biscuits, we will discover the secrets of the legendary art of MURANO GLASSMAKING.

• Walking on water

High water is a natural phenomenon that occurs very frequently in Venice, especially in autumn and winter. When particular atmospheric conditions are added to tidal waves, flooding occurs in various parts of the city. For this reason, Venetians have an efficient system of wooden walkways that make it possible to "walk on water."

• The MOSE system

To protect Venice from the high water, a large system of mobile floodgates has been designed. Imagine gigantic steel gates positioned under the sea, which lift like shields, stopping the rising water.

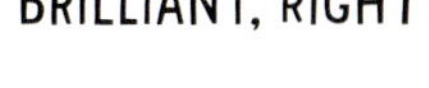

BRILLIANT, RIGHT?

GIUDECCA

All aboard, little explorers. We are sailing for Spinalonga!

This was the name of the island of Giudecca in the past. And do you know why? Because of its shape, naturally! If you looked at it from above, you would see that it looks like a *spina di pesce*, a fish bone made of eight small islands connected by bridges. To get there we must take the *vaporetto*, but just once a year it can be reached on foot.

During the Feast of the Redeemer, which is held on the third Sunday in July, a SPECIAL BRIDGE made of boats is "constructed"!

• A delicious mission

This enchanting island is the ideal place to stroll, go in search of small secret gardens hidden among the streets, visit the shops of artisans, and...eat the famous *Gianduiotto di Nico* in front of the Fondamenta delle Zattere.

It is a slice of gianduja (a mix of chocolate and hazelnuts) served in a layer of whipped cream.

SLURP, MY MOUTH IS ALREADY WATERING!

SAN GIORGIO MAGGIORE

Are you ready for an adventure between sky and land?

Right next to Giudecca there is another small island on which the bell tower of the basilica stands out like a lighthouse.

IT IS 246 FEET (75 METERS) HIGH, AND FROM UP THERE THE VIEW IS REALLY MAGNIFICENT.

- **The Borges Labyrinth**

On the island there is a labyrinth made up of 3,250 boxwoods interwoven to form the name of Borges, a writer who loved Venice. But that is not all!

Within the labyrinth items that Borges held dear are hidden.

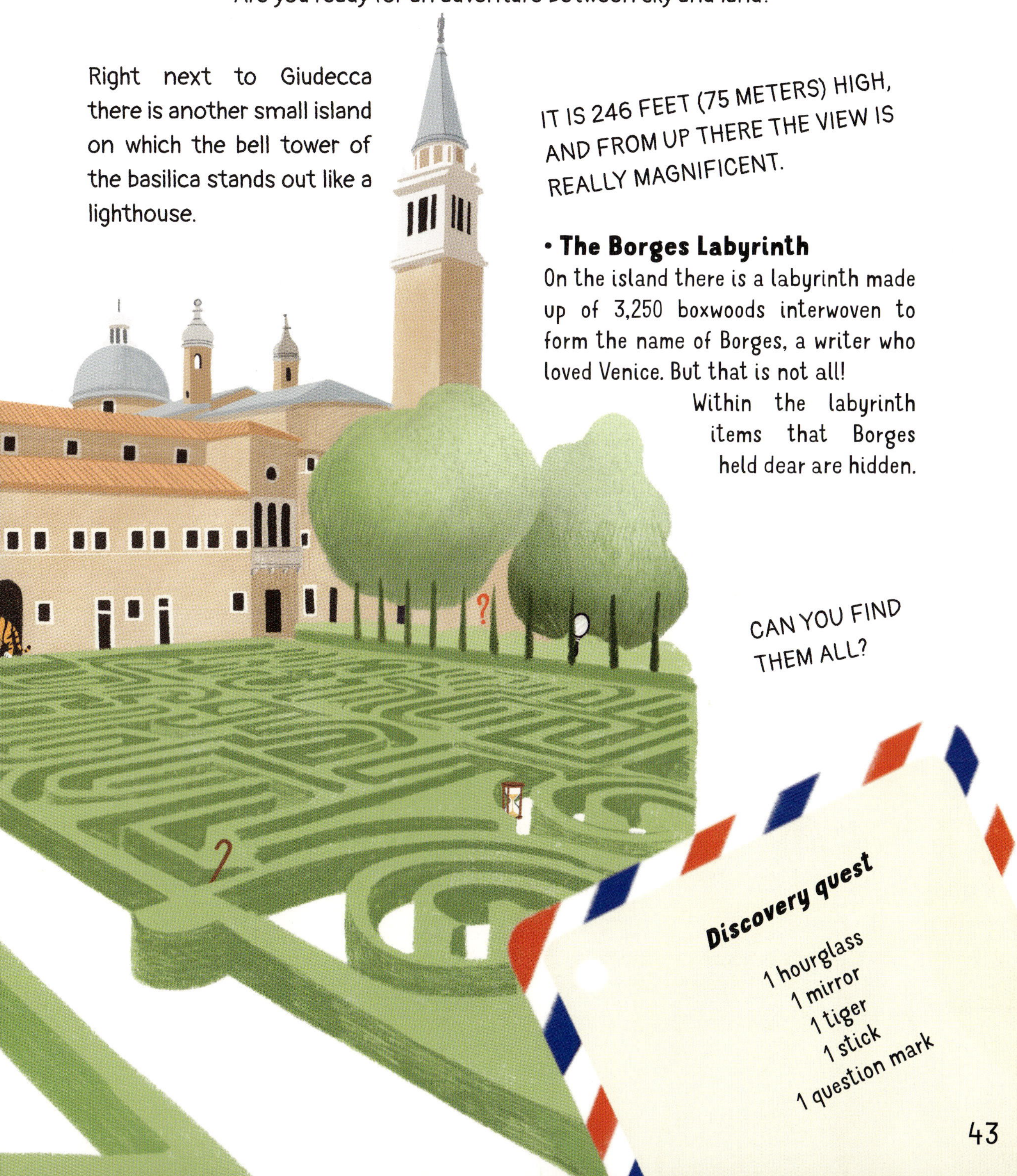

CAN YOU FIND THEM ALL?

Discovery quest

1 hourglass
1 mirror
1 tiger
1 stick
1 question mark

BURANO

Welcome to the most colorful island of the lagoon!

Doesn't it look like you are entering a box of colored pencils? Burano's houses are red and pink, orange and yellow, and all the colors of the rainbow.

It is said that the fishermen returning home in the fog could easily find their house, but also that, having to paint them often because of the humidity, the women would mix any color available.

• Bepi's house

Behind the Piazza di Burano there is a rather special house, brightly colored and decorated with geometric shapes. It is the house of *Giuseppe Toselli*, a painting enthusiast who in the evening would hang a sheet on the facade to project cartoons to make the children happy.

• The *campanil storto*

Even the bell tower of the church is special in Burano because it is crooked. Due to the sinking of the land, it has tilted by 6 feet (1.83 meters)!

AND NOW WHAT DO YOU THINK ABOUT TASTING A WONDERFUL *BUSSOLÀ*, THE TRADITIONAL BISCUIT OF BURANO? I LOVE IT!

MURANO

Let's go and discover the secrets of glassmaking!

Composed of seven small islands connected by bridges, Murano is famous all over the world for the production of BLOWN GLASS. For almost a millennium, MASTER GLASSBLOWERS have transformed sand and fire into extraordinary colored works of art.

Just imagine that at one time, Venice was so jealous of this unique and extraordinary art that in order to leave the island, the glassmakers needed a special permit!

• Fire, breath, and imagination

On Murano it is possible to visit one of the many KILNS, the places where the glass comes to life. The masters take the molten glass from the kiln, which stays on night and day, and with long iron rods they shape it and blow it, and from an incandescent mass they create the most wonderful shapes: cats, fish, gondolas, jewels, and even lions!

• An ancient recipe

The typical sweet of Murano is the *bussolà*. Unlike the one from Burano, it is enriched with dried and candied fruit, chocolate, and spices.

ROAR!
I CAN'T STOP!

WELL MY FRIENDS, WITH MY MANE FULL OF CRUMBS I SALUTE YOU. I HOPE YOU HAD FUN TRAVELING WITH ME.

CONTINUE TO EXPLORE THE WORLD, AND ALWAYS KEEP YOUR IMAGINATION ALIVE LIKE THE FIRE IN THE MURANO KILNS.

GOODBYE!

LAURA RE

Born in Rome, Laura attended the *Scuola Romana del Fumetto*. She later collaborated with animation studios in the role of character designer, concept artist, and illustrator. After attending the International School of Illustration in Sarmede, she moved to Milan to complete the Illustration Master Class at Mimaster. There she deepened her knowledge of publishing and illustration for children.

DANIELA CELLI

Born in Florence in 1977, Daniela studied piano at the "Luigi Cherubini" Conservatory before moving to New York to study criminology. She returned to Italy in 1997 and graduated with a degree in law while also obtaining a diploma at the *Accademia d'Arte Drammatica*. A long-time travel enthusiast, she has been blogging about adventures with her family around the world since 2008.

Graphic layout: Valentina Figus

SIOR LEO

Distant cousin of the legendary lion of Saint Mark, he decided to leave his job as a statue to take children around Venice. He once had wings, but he lost them in a diving competition off the Bridge of Sighs. Since then he has moved around by *vaporetto*, always with a bag of *bussolà* and a mane full of crumbs.

Piazzale Luigi Cadorna, 6 - 20123 Milan, Italy
www.whitestar.it

Translation: Qontent
Editing: Michele Suchomel-Casey

First printing, March 2026

ISBN 978-88-544-2188-2
1 2 3 4 5 6   30 29 28 27 26

Printed and manufactured in China by Shenzhen Dream Colour Printing Company Limited, Shenzhen, Guangdong